GEORGE WASHINGTON

Leni Donlan

Raintree

Chicago, Illinois

© 2007 Raintree
Published by Raintree,
A division of Reed Elsevier Inc.
Chicago, Illinois

Customer Service 888-363-4266

Visit our website at www.heinemannraintree.com

Designed by Michelle Lisseter, Kim Miracle,
and Bigtop
Printed in China

10 09 08
10 9 8 7 6 5 4 3 2

**Library of Congress
Cataloging-in-Publication Data**
Donlan, Leni.
George Washington : revolution and the new nation
/ Leni Donlan.
        p. cm. -- (American history through primary
sources)
  Includes bibliographical references and index.
  ISBN 1-4109-2420-3 (hc) -- ISBN 1-4109-2431-9 (pb)
 1. Washington, George, 1732-1799--Juvenile
literature. 2.
Presidents--United States--Biography--Juvenile
literature. 3.
Generals--United States--Biography--Juvenile
literature. 4. United
States--History--Revolution, 1775-1783--Juvenile
literature. 5. United
States--History--Colonial period, ca. 1600-1775--
Juvenile literature. 6.
United States--History--Confederation, 1783-1789--
Juvenile literature. I.
Title. II. Series.
  E312.66.D66 2007
  973.4'1092--dc22
  [B]
                                      2006010664
13-digit ISBNs
978-1-4109-2420-9 (hardcover)
978-1-4109-2431-5 (paperback)

Acknowledgments
The author and publisher are grateful to the
following for permission to reproduce copyright
material: The Granger Collection, New York **p. 27**;
Library of Congress Geography and Map Division
p. 5; Library of Congress Manuscript Division **p. 23**;
Library of Congress Prints and Photographs Division
pp. 6, **7**, **9**, **10**, **11**, **13**, **14**, **15**, **17**, **19**, **21**, **22**, **25**,
26, **28**, **29** **(all)**.

Cover photograph of the inauguration of George
Washington as the first president of the United States
reproduced with permission of The Granger
Collection, New York.

Photo research by Tracy Cummins.

Illustrations by Darren Lingard.

The publishers would like to thank Nancy Harris and
Joy Rogers for their assistance in the preparation of
this book.

Every effort has been made to contact copyright
holders of any material reproduced in this book. Any
omissions will be rectified in subsequent printings if
notice is given to the publishers.

Disclaimer
All the Internet addresses (URLs) given in this book
were valid at the time of going to press. However, due
to the dynamic nature of the Internet, some addresses
may have changed, or sites may have changed or
ceased to exist since publication. While the author and
publishers regret any inconvenience this may cause
readers, no responsibility for any such changes can be
accepted by either the author or the publishers.

It is recommended that adults should supervise
children on the Internet.

Contents

Some words are printed in bold, **like this**. You can find out what they mean on page 30. You can also look in the box at the bottom of the page where they first appear.

The North American Colonies

A **colony** is a group of people. These people live far from their home country. Although far away, they are still ruled by their home country.

In 1750 there were thirteen colonies. These were on the east coast of North America (see map on page 5). The colonies were ruled by Great Britain. Great Britain is a large island in Europe. It is separated from North America by an ocean. It is 3,000 miles (4,800 kilometers) away!

Colonists are people who live in a colony. Colonists came to North America for a better life. The colonists thought of themselves as British. (A person who lives in Great Britain is called British.) But the colonists lived in North America now. The colonists began to see themselves as Americans, too.

Great Britain thought the colonists should obey British rules. Yet the colonists did not want Britain telling them what to do. Trouble was coming.

colonist   person who lives in a colony
colony   group of people who live far away from their home
               country, but are still ruled by their home country

▼ *This is a map of the North American colonies. It was made in 1755.*

George Washington of Virginia

George Washington was born on February 22, 1732. He was born in the North American **colony** of Virginia. His parents gave him a nice home. They gave him a good education.

After his father died, George went to live with his brother. George loved his brother's home. It was called Mount Vernon. Then, George's brother died. George became the owner of Mount Vernon.

Young George Washington leads friends in a game of war. ▶

surveyor	person who studies an area to find the size, shape, and angle of the land
widow	woman whose husband has died

George married Martha Custis in 1759. Martha was a young **widow**. A widow is a woman whose husband has died. She had two children. George, Martha, and her children led a happy life together at Mount Vernon.

George was big and strong. He was more than six feet tall. He had blue-gray eyes and dark red hair. George was a quiet man. He spoke only when he had something important to say. When people met George, they usually liked and admired him.

A surveyor

As a young man, George Washington learned to be a **surveyor**. A surveyor studies an area to find the size, shape, and angle of the land.

▼George Washington marries Martha Custis.

Trouble in the Colonies

In 1760 King George III became the king of Great Britain. He was not popular in Great Britain. He was even less popular in the North American **colonies**.

Benjamin Franklin lived in the colonies. He was a very smart man. He made people laugh. He also made them think. Franklin said:

"We have an old mother that peevish [irritable] is grown;
She snubs [ignores] us like children that scarce walk alone;
She forgets we're grown up and have sense of our own."

It sounds like a family fight, doesn't it? Who are the children? Who is the old mother?

To be fair, King George III had some big problems in the colonies. He had a lot to worry about. King George thought Great Britain had to manage all the people in the thirteen North American colonies. He also thought he had to keep the **colonists** and the Native Americans from fighting with each other.

▲This is King George III of Great Britain. He wears a fur robe and a powdered wig.

A Proclamation and Some Acts

King George III continued to make the **colonists** angry. First, he issued a **proclamation** (order). It was called the Proclamation of 1763. It ordered Native Americans and colonists to live in different places.

The colonists did not like being told where to live. They also did not like getting orders from a king who lived far away. The colonists ignored the king's proclamation.

Then, the king made laws, or "acts." They were made to get money from the colonists. First came the Stamp Act. Colonists had to pay **taxes** when they bought paper. Taxes are money collected by the **government**. The government is the group of people who run a country.

A skull and crossbones ▶ mean danger or death. The colonists' use of this image shows how much they disliked the Stamp Act.

government	group of people who run a country
harbor	part of a body of water where ships load and unload
proclamation	announcement of an order
tax	money collected by a government

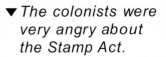

11

Next, the king tried to tax tea. The American people showed how angry they were. They climbed aboard the ships that carried tea. They threw the tea into Boston **Harbor** (where the ships sat). This event was called the Boston Tea Party. The year was 1773.

Enough!

Then, King George III made the **colonists** angry again. The British punished the people of Boston for their "Tea Party." The British **blockaded** Boston **Harbor**. This means they stopped ships from coming in or leaving the harbor.

Great Britain sent soldiers to North America. The colonists were expected to **quarter** the soldiers. This means they had to give the soldiers a place to live. Americans did not want to quarter British soldiers. The people in Boston refused.

In March of 1770, something terrible happened in Boston. Americans were making fun of a British soldier. Then, they started pushing and shoving. Next, a British soldier fired his gun. Other soldiers fired, too. The Americans did not have weapons. Five Americans died. Six more were wounded. This was called the Boston **Massacre**. A massacre is the violent and cruel killing of people.

blockade	to close off a waterway, such as a harbor or river
massacre	violent and cruel killing of people
quarter	to provide a place to live

The BLOODY MASSACRE perpetrated in King Street

▼ This is a famous picture of the Boston Massacre.

Americans wanted the British to stop giving them orders. The British wanted to make the Americans behave. The British and the Americans were fed up with each other!

Breaking Away from Britain

American leaders thought that the **colonies** should break free from Britain.

In 1774 a group met in Philadelphia. The group was called the Continental Congress. They decided to give King George one last chance. They sent a **petition** (a written request) to the king. They asked for freedom from British rule.

The Continental Congress made plans to meet again. They planned to meet after the king received the petition. The group hoped King George would listen.

Thomas Paine

*Thomas Paine was a newcomer to North America. He was a writer. His writing showed people it was time to break free from British rule. Paine did not like a **government** that was led by a king or queen. He said that it was unfair for Americans to pay **taxes** to Great Britain. He said it was silly for Americans to obey a country that was 3,000 miles (4,800 kilometers) away.*

liberty   freedom
petition   formal, written request

▼ Patrick Henry said, "Give me **liberty** or give me death!" He was willing to die to be free from British rule.

The British Are Coming

King George III did not pay attention to the **petition**. Americans knew that British soldiers would be coming. They began hiding and moving **ammunition**. The ammunition was gunpowder and cannonballs. They stored the ammunition in the small town of Concord. Concord is near the city of Boston.

Paul Revere was a **colonist**. He overheard a British plan. British soldiers were going to march to Concord. They were going to take the Americans' ammunition.

Revere sent spies to find out which way the British soldiers would travel. One spy went up in the tower of the North Church in Boston. If the soldiers were going to Concord by land, the spy would light one lantern. If the soldiers were going to Concord by sea, the spy would light two lanterns.

Revere watched. He saw the light of two lanterns. He knew that the British were going by sea! Another man named William Dawes joined him. Revere and Dawes borrowed horses. They raced through the night. As they rode, they cried out, "The British are coming!"

ammunition   gunpowder and cannonballs

▼On the morning of April 19, 1775, an alarm was rung. It rang from this tower in Lexington, Massachusetts. It told people that the British were coming.

17

The shot heard round the world

Henry Wadsworth Longfellow was a famous American writer. He wrote a poem about Paul Revere's ride. He wrote about the lights in the North church tower in Boston. He wrote:

Listen, my children, and you shall hear
Of the midnight ride of Paul Revere,
On the eighteenth of April, in seventy-five;
Hardly a man is now alive
Who remembers that famous day and year.
And lo! as he looks, on the belfry's [tower's] height
A glimmer and then a gleam of light!
He springs to the saddle, the bridle he turns,
But lingers and gazes till full on his sight
A second lamp in the belfry burns!

The American soldiers were called minutemen. The British soldiers were called redcoats. This was because they wore bright red uniforms. On April 19, 1775, the minutemen and redcoats exchanged shots. The American War of **Revolution** had begun. A revolution is a change in **government**. Americans wanted their own leaders to run the country.

revolution   change in government

▲The minutemen were farmers. They could grab their guns and be ready to fight in just a minute!

Another poet, Ralph Waldo Emerson, added to Longfellow's poem. His last line became famous. This is Emerson's famous last line:

...And fired the shot heard round the world.

Why do you think Emerson described it as "the shot heard round the world"?

The Second Continental Congress

Once again, Americans came to meet in Philadelphia. They were **delegates**. A delegate is a person who stands in for and acts for others.

George Washington and Benjamin Franklin were delegates in Philadelphia. So were Thomas Jefferson and John Adams.

John Adams talked with the other delegates. He told them that battles like those of Concord and Lexington could happen anywhere. He said the **colonies** needed an army. They also needed a general to lead the army.

Adams suggested George Washington for that position. Washington agreed. Washington set off to take charge of American soldiers.

declaration	written statement
delegate	person who stands in for and acts for others
independence	freedom from the control of someone else

The Continental Congress wrote one more **petition** (request) to King George III. They asked for freedom from British rule. The delegates still hoped to avoid war if they could.

They also started writing a **Declaration** of **Independence**. A declaration is a written statement. Independence meant being free from the rule of Great Britain.

The Colonies Declare Independence

Thomas Jefferson was asked to write the **Declaration** of **Independence**. He wrote about what King George did wrong. He wrote about what a good **government** should do. (A government is a group of people who run a country.) Jefferson wrote that the **colonies** were free from Britain.

The declaration said: "All men are created equal, and have certain unalienable, [unchangeable] rights that include: life, **liberty** [freedom], and the pursuit [the following] of happiness."

▼Thomas Jefferson, Benjamin Franklin, and John Adams are busy writing the Declaration of Independence.

The declaration also said that people should vote for their government. The government is for the people. It must do what the people want it to do.

On July 4, 1776, the Second Continental Congress met. They approved the Declaration of Independence. Most **delegates** (representatives) signed the declaration. This made them **traitors** against Britain. A traitor is someone who turns against his or her country. If they were caught, the British could hang them.

▲This is an early copy of the Declaration of Independence. It was changed many times.

traitor   person who betrays his or her country

A Leader in War

George Washington was made leader of the American army. Two days later, the Americans and British were fighting. The first battle was in Boston.

The British army had many more soldiers. It had more weapons. It had more **ammunition** (gunpowder and cannonballs). The British won the battle. But more than 1,000 British soldiers were killed or wounded. The Americans lost 400 soldiers that day.

When the war started, American soldiers had no training. They did not have proper uniforms. They did not have enough supplies. There were less American soldiers than British soldiers.

The Americans were not expected to win this war. But they were brave. They were fighting for their country. This made them tough and strong.

It was a long, hard war. It lasted eight years. Both sides won and lost battles. The American army finally defeated the British army. On October 19, 1781, the war was over. The North American **colonies** had won against huge odds.

General Washington was an▼ excellent leader. He and his army fought many battles. They did not give up!

A Leader for a New Nation

In May of 1787, **delegates** (representatives) met again in Philadelphia. George Washington led this meeting.

They made a blueprint (plan) for our country. It was called the Constitution of the United States. It has served the country well for over 200 years.

People from thirteen different **colonies** became united as one country. They became the United States of America. All the delegates chose George Washington to be the first president of the United States.

▼ *This photo shows the delegates signing the U.S. Constitution. George Washington is seated in the chair.*

▲ George Washington becomes the first president of the United States.

Washington agreed to serve. He would have preferred to go home to Martha and Mount Vernon. Washington was president for eight years.

Washington was a good leader in peace. He had been a good leader in war, too. The American people loved him. He is remembered as the father of the United States.

The Signers

These brave men signed the ▲
Declaration of **Independence**.
They became **traitors** to King
George III and Great Britain. They
risked their lives. They wanted to
be free men in a free country.

Benjamin Franklin

(1706–1790)

Benjamin Franklin was a businessman, writer, scientist, and statesman. A **statesman** is a person involved in matters of government. Franklin helped write the Declaration of Independence.

John Hancock

(1737–1793)

John Hancock is famous for his signature. It is the biggest and boldest signature on the Declaration of Independence.

John Adams

(1735–1826)

John Adams was the first vice president of the United States. He was the second president. He was a strong supporter of the Declaration of Independence.

Thomas Jefferson

(1743–1826)

Thomas Jefferson was a lawyer, musician, scientist, author, and inventor. He was also the third president of the United States. He wrote the Declaration of Independence.

statesman   person involved in matters of government

Glossary

ammunition gunpowder and cannonballs

blockade to close off a waterway, such as a harbor or river

colonist person who lives in a colony

colony group of people who live far away from their home country, but are still ruled by their home country

declaration written statement

delegate person who stands in for and acts for others

government group of people who run a country

harbor part of a body of water where ships load and unload

independence freedom from the control of someone else

liberty freedom

massacre violent and cruel killing of people

petition formal, written request

proclamation announcement of an order

quarter to provide a place to live

revolution change in government

statesman person involved in matters of government

surveyor person who studies an area to find the size, shape, and angle of the land

tax money collected by a government

traitor person who betrays his or her country

widow woman whose husband has died

Want to Know More?

Books to read

- Burke, Rick. *George Washington*. Chicago: Heinemann Library, 2003.

- Fritz, Jean. *And Then What Happened, Paul Revere?* New York: Putnam, 1996.

- Smolinski, Diane. *Important People of the Revolutionary War*. Chicago: Heinemann Library, 2002.

Websites

- http://www.americaslibrary.gov/ cgi-bin/page.cgi/aa/presidents/wash
  Learn more about George Washington at this Library of Congress site.

- http://www.americaslibrary.gov/ cgi-bin/page.cgi/jb/revolut
  Learn more about the period of U.S. history from 1764 to 1789 at this Library of Congress site.

- http://www.americaslibrary.gov/ cgi-bin/page.cgi/jb/nation
  Learn more about the period of U.S. history from 1790 to 1828 at this Library of Congress site.

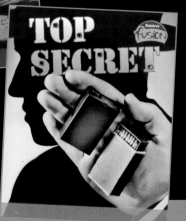

Read ***The Dirty Thirties: Documenting the Dust Bowl*** to learn about the dust storms that swept across the midwestern United States during the 1930s.

Read ***Top Secret: Spy Equipment and the Cold War*** to explore the mysterious world of spies.

Index